Leaders of New York's Industrial Growth

James Bernard

New York

Published in 2015 by The Rosen Publishing Group, Inc.
29 East 21st Street, New York, NY 10010

Book Design: Chris Brand

Photo Credits: Cover, pp. 5, 7 (left insert), 13, 19 © Bettmann/Corbis; pp. 7, 9 (inset) © Corbis; pp. 7 (right insert), 15 (left inset) © Hulton/Archive; pp. 9, 11 (inset), 21 (left inset) Library of Congress Prints and Photographs Division, Washington, D.C.; p. 11 Getty Images; p. 15 (right inset) Science & Society Picture Library/SSPL/Getty Images; p. 15 Shutterstock.com; p. 17 (both) © Queens Borough Public Library, Long Island Division, Latimer Family Papers; p. 19 (inset) © Hulton-Deutsch Collection/Corbis; p. 21 (right inset) Hulton Archive/Getty Images; p. 21 ChameleonsEye/Shutterstock.com.

Library of Congress Cataloging-in-Publication Data

Bernard, James.
Leaders of New York's industrial growth / by James Bernard.
p. cm. — (Spotlight on New York)
Includes index.
ISBN 978-1-4777-7338-3 (pbk.)
ISBN 978-1-4777-6416-9 (6-pack)
ISBN 978-1-4777-7323-9 (library binding)
1. Economic development—New York (State)—Juvenile literature. 2. Industrialization—New York (State)—History—Juvenile literature. 3. New York (State)—History— Juvenile literature. I. Bernard, James. II. Title.
HC107.N7 B47 2015
338.9747—d23

Manufactured in the United States of America

CPSIA Compliance Information: Batch #WS15RC: For further information contact Rosen Publishing, New York, New York at 1-800-237-9932.

Contents

An Industrial Economy

The nineteenth century was a period of rapid growth and change in the United States. The changes brought on by the **Industrial Revolution** made it faster, easier, and cheaper to **manufacture** goods. The national **economy** changed from one based on agriculture to one based on **industry**.

America's growing industrial economy required a lot of support. Railroads were needed to move goods and **raw materials** across the expanding country. The railroad industry needed a constant supply of wood, steel, and **coal** to run efficiently. Oil was needed for the machines that ran **factories**. Companies that were able to supply the things that America's growing economy needed grew wealthy.

During this period, New York State truly came into its own as a center for industry and economy. Local businessmen, inventors, **engineers**, and **architects** helped New York grow and prosper. Many of the advances and **innovations** that first occurred in New York State spread to other parts of the country, changing life in America forever.

As the economy of New York State grew, so did greed and dishonesty. Working and living conditions got worse for poor people. Many factories, like the one shown here, used child labor and paid the children very little. Slums—crowded areas in cities where poverty and unhealthy living conditions are common—grew larger as people grew poorer.

The Business of Railroads

Railroads were very important to the growing businesses in New York. Cornelius Vanderbilt was a shipping and railroad businessman. He built **steamboat** and railroad routes around New York City and across New York State. Vanderbilt created the New York Central Railroad that connected New York City, Albany, and Buffalo. Soon this railroad would connect New York State to other states like Illinois and Missouri. Connecting New York City to the rest of the state and country made it easier to buy and sell products. That helped the economy of New York State to grow.

Jay Gould was a businessman from New York. He became wealthy and powerful by buying and selling railroads. In 1869, Gould and his partners took control of the **gold market**. They bought all the gold they could in New York. That way they could control the price. Gould and his partners grew rich, but many other businessmen lost money.

In the late 1860s, Vanderbilt and Gould fought for control of New York State's Erie Railroad. Gould won because of the unfair way he did business. Men who became rich doing business this way were called "robber barons." The photo shows the New York Elevated Railroad and the Staten Island Ferry Terminal in the 1890s.

Jay Gould

Cornelius Vanderbilt

7

Building the Brooklyn Bridge

John Augustus Roebling was an engineer and inventor. In 1831, he came to the United States from Germany. He helped to plan and build canals. Roebling also invented a wire cable that was strong enough to pull boats and train engines without breaking. Roebling began to use his cable for building bridges. These were called **suspension bridges**.

In 1867, he drew up a plan for a bridge that would cross the East River in New York, connecting Brooklyn and Manhattan. At the time, Manhattan and Brooklyn were two separate cities. The construction of the Brooklyn Bridge made it easier for these two cities to become one in 1898.

Roebling died in 1869 and his son, Washington, took over the project. Washington Roebling was injured during the construction and had to supervise the workers from a house in Brooklyn Heights. His wife, Emily Roebling, carried messages between her husband and the workers. Roebling's Brooklyn Bridge opened in 1883. It made travel between the two places much easier.

The Brooklyn Bridge was one of the largest bridges in the world when it was completed in 1883. In 1964, the National Park Service made the Brooklyn Bridge a national historic landmark. This picture shows the Brooklyn Bridge around 1883, shortly after it was finished.

John Augustus Roebling

City of Glass

Amory Houghton was a businessman who owned a glass factory in Brooklyn, New York. In 1868, he moved his factory to Corning, a city in south central New York. He renamed the company the Corning Glass Works. Making glass requires a lot of heat. Corning was close to the railroad, making it easy to get coal to the factory for its furnaces. It was also near the Chemung River, which provided access to both the Great Lakes region and the Atlantic Ocean. The company made a new lamp out of stronger glass so the railroad's lights would last longer.

In 1908, the Corning Glass Works opened one of the first glass **research labs** in America. Many important inventions have come from this lab, including a new form of science called fiber optics, which shines light along very thin glass threads to **transmit** pictures. Fiber optics are used in medicine, computers, and television. In 1990, Corning produced the glass used to make the mirror in the Hubble Space Telescope. Today, the Corning Museum of Glass brings many visitors to the state.

In 1880, Corning Glass Works began to make lightbulbs, like the one seen here, for Thomas Edison's new electric lamps. The factory produced lightbulbs at the rate of 1,200 per day. By 1926, Corning Glass Works had invented a machine to make bulbs more quickly and cheaply, so that almost everyone could afford them. Today, this machine can make 2,000 bulbs each minute! The smaller picture shows a Corning worker molding glass in 1943.

The Oil Industry

During the Industrial Revolution, oil was an important source of **fuel**. It was used to run machines in factories, and later it was used to help run cars. In 1870, a New Yorker named John Davison Rockefeller started the Standard Oil Company in Ohio. He built **oil wells** and **pipelines** all over the country. By 1882, Rockefeller and his partners controlled much of the oil trade in the world. They were accused of using unfair methods that hurt other businesses. The company had to be broken down into smaller companies. Many of these still exist today.

Rockefeller and his partners became rich from the oil trade. Rockefeller used much of his money to help other people. He set up several important **charities**. He donated about $540 million to many different causes to try to fix many of the problems he saw in the world around him, such as housing for the poor. Rockefeller created the Rockefeller Foundation, the first global **philanthropic** organization. He helped make important changes to New York City's police departments, schools, and public health system.

In 1901, Rockefeller founded the Rockefeller Institute for Medical Research (renamed Rockefeller University in 1965). It brought talented scientists to New York. Many important discoveries were made at the institute, including a cure for a terrible disease called yellow fever.

13

The War of Currents

In the late 1880s, Thomas Edison developed a system to transmit electricity using direct current. Direct current transmits electricity in one direction. Edison opened the first **power plant** on Pearl Street in New York City in 1882. Edison's Pearl Street Station began generating electricity on September 4, 1882, providing electricity to 59 customers in lower Manhattan.

Edison's direct current was not the only method of transmitting electricity. Nikola Tesla, a Serbian inventor and engineer, believed that using an alternating current would be better than Edison's direct current. An alternating current changes direction, which means the electricity can be transmitted using cheaper wires and over longer distances.

Tesla's ideas inspired American inventor George Westinghouse, who used Tesla's alternating current to found the Westinghouse Electric Company. His company created a way to use water to power things. Westinghouse opened the Niagara Falls Power Company in 1895. It generated enough electricity to light Buffalo. Alternating current is still used today to transmit electricity to our homes and businesses. Direct current still exists today in the form of batteries and in **solar cells**.

George Westinghouse

Nikola Tesla

This photo shows Niagara Falls today. In 1896, Westinghouse's company turned waterpower from Niagara Falls into electric energy. Niagara Falls provided a large supply of low-cost, water-driven power, and it attracted many industries to nearby Buffalo.

Draftsman and Inventor

Lewis Howard Latimer was one of the few African American inventors of his time. His parents had been **slaves**. He started working in Boston. There, he taught himself how to be a **draftsman**, which meant he drew plans for machines. In 1874, he invented a new part for toilets on trains. He also invented an early air conditioning unit. He invented a part that made electric lightbulbs shine brighter and last longer. He led the team who set up the first electric streetlights in New York and other cities.

Latimer worked closely with Alexander Graham Bell, helping draft the **patent** for Bell's invention: the telephone. In 1884, Latimer moved to New York to work for Thomas Edison at the Edison Electric Light Company. He played an important role in protecting Edison's patents. He also worked at the Henry Street Settlement in Manhattan. He taught immigrants how to be draftsmen. He continued to invent for the rest of his life.

Shown here is the patent for one of Latimer's inventions—a locking rack for hats, coats, and umbrellas.

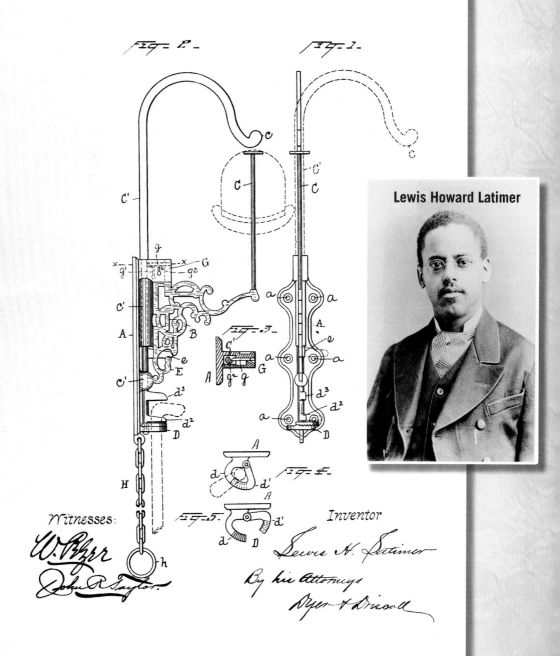

(No Model.)

L. H. LATIMER.

LOCKING RACK FOR HATS, COATS, UMBRELLAS, &c.

No. 557,076.

Patented Mar. 24, 1896.

Lewis Howard Latimer

Witnesses:

Inventor

Photographs and Copies

In the early 1800s, flour milling was the most important industry in Rochester, New York. However, the Eastman Kodak Company made Rochester famous. In 1883, George Eastman invented roll film and changed photography forever. Early cameras had taken pictures on specially prepared glass plates that were heavy and hard to use. Each picture required a new plate, so photographers had to carry many plates. Eastman's roll film was flexible, light, and easy to carry. In 1888, he invented the Kodak camera. The roll film and Kodak camera were so easy to use that anyone could take pictures.

Founded in Rochester in 1906, the Haloid Company made photographic paper. In 1938, a scientist named Chester Carlson invented a way of using **static electricity** to print images. In 1947, the Haloid Company, now called the Xerox Corporation, used this method to create a machine that could make exact copies of documents. The company's Xerox machine made office work faster and easier.

George Eastman's company made cameras that were inexpensive and easy to use. This helped make photography a popular hobby enjoyed by millions of people. The famous Kodak motto, or saying, appears in the upper left corner of the Kodak advertisement on the opposite page: "You press the button, we do the rest."

George Eastman

"You press the button We do the rest"

Jack: Do you think baby will be quiet long enough to take her picture, mamma?

Mamma: The Kodak will catch her whether she moves or not ; it is as "quick as a wink."

Send to the Eastman Company, Rochester, N. Y., for a copy of "Do I want a Camera," (illustrated) free by mail.

Investment Banking and Finance

Factory owners and inventors often needed a lot of money. National banks could not keep up with the sudden need for large amounts of money. Investment banks helped businesses in need of money find willing **investors**. Investors share in the profits of businesses that they invest in, so it was important to invest in businesses that they felt would be successful.

J.P. Morgan was the son of a banker. In 1857, Morgan began working at the London branch of his father's bank, Peabody, Morgan, and Company. Morgan invested in many growing industries of the day. He financed numerous steel and iron businesses like the Federal Steel Company. Morgan was also a **benefactor** of the American Museum of Natural History and the Metropolitan Museum of Art, both located in New York City.

At a time when most wealthy investors were men, Hetty Green was known as "the richest woman in America." Green became wealthy investing in railroads, mines, and real estate. At the time of her death, Green was worth about $200 million.

In addition to being a banker and wealthy businessman, J.P. Morgan also helped establish the Metropolitan Museum of Art, seen here. Morgan was not alone. Many of the nineteenth century's wealthiest individuals contributed to libraries, museums, hospitals, and universities.

J.P. Morgan

Hetty Green

Industry in New York

New York businessmen and inventors from the late 1800s and early 1900s changed the way people do things across the country. Their **influence** is still felt today. The Rockefeller Foundation continues to carry out the charitable work of John D. Rockefeller. A public school in Brooklyn is named after Lewis Howard Latimer. George Eastman founded the Eastman School of Music in Rochester, one of the best in the country. Every day, more than 140,000 people move through Grand Central Station, built by Cornelius Vanderbilt in 1871.

New York State is still a world leader in industry today. Printed materials, clothing, and food are all manufactured in New York. New York is also a leading producer of machines for electronics, computers, and **transportation**.

New York City is a center of finance, art, mass media, and journalism. In 2006, Google opened an office in New York City. With over 500 employees, it is the largest office outside of Google's main headquarters in California.

Glossary

architect: Someone who designs buildings.

benefactor: A person who helps an institution by giving money.

charities: Organizations that are started to help those in need.

coal: A natural resource that can be burned to create energy.

draftsman: A person who draws plans for machines.

economy: The production and use of goods and services.

engineer: A person trained to use scientific knowledge to solve practical problems.

factories: Manufacturing plants.

fuel: A substance that can be used to produce energy.

gold market: The buying and selling of the world's supply of gold.

Industrial Revolution: The period in history when the means of production shifted from hand tools to power-driven machines.

industry: Businesses that provide a certain product or service.

influence: To have a lasting effect on.

innovations: New ideas, devices, or ways of doing something.

investors: Someone who supplies money to a business in return for a share of the profits.

manufacture: Produce by hand or by machine.

oil wells: A hole drilled into the earth from which oil is pumped.

patents: Official documents granting an inventor the sole rights to their invention.

philanthropic: Showing concern for humanity, especially by donating money.

pipelines: A system of pipes used to transport liquids or gases.

power plant: A building or group of buildings in which electricity for a large area is produced.

raw materials: Materials that are manufactured into goods.

research labs: A workplace where scientists make new discoveries.

slaves: People who are owned by another person and forced to work without getting paid.

solar cells: Devices that convert energy from sunlight into electrical energy.

static electricity: Electricity created by rubbing two objects together.

steamboats: Boats powered by a steam engine.

suspension bridges: Bridges that have a roadway and are supported by cables that are anchored at both ends.

transmit: To send from one place to another.

transportation: The act of moving something from one location to another.

Index

Primary Source List

Page 5. *Children working spinning machines textile mill.* Photograph. ca. 1909.

Page 7 (left inset). *Jay Gould.* Published by Bain News Service. Glass negative. ca. 1880s. Now kept at the Library of Congress Prints and Photographs Division, Washington, DC.

Page 7. *Elevated Railroad at Staten Island Ferry Terminal.* Photograph. ca. 1890s.

Page 9. *The great East River suspension bridge—Connecting the cities of New York and Brooklyn.* Printed by Currier & Ives. Lithograph. ca. 1874. Now kept at the Library of Congress Prints and Photographs Division, Washington, DC.

Page 9 (inset). *John August Roebling.* Sketch based on Gelatin silver print. Between 1866 and 1867. Now kept at the Brooklyn Museum, New York, NY.

Page 11 (inset). *Corning Glass Works, Parkersburg, West Virginia, February 18, 1943.* Photograph. Now kept at the Library of Congress Prints and Photographs Division, Washington, DC.

Page 15 (left inset). *George Westinghouse, half-length portrait, facing front.* Photograph by Joseph G. Gessford. Photographic print. Between 1900 and 1914. Now kept at the Library of Congress Prints and Photographs Division, Washington, DC.

Page 15 (right inset). *Nicola Tesla.* Published by Bain News Service. Glass negative. Now kept at the Library of Congress Prints and Photographs Division, Washington, DC.

Page 17 (inset). *Lewis Howard Latimer.* Photograph by Mitchell Photography Studio on High Street in London Borough of Lewisham. Photographic print. 1882. Now part of the Latimer Family Papers, Queens Borough Public Library, Long Island Division, New York, NY.

Page 17. *Patent drawing of Locking Rack for Hats, Coats, and Umbrellas.* Created by Lewis Howard Latimer. Blue print drawings. Now part of the Latimer Family Papers, Queens Borough Public Library, Long Island Division, New York, NY.

Page 19 (inset). *George Eastman.* Photograph. ca. 1900. Now kept at International Museum of Photography and Film at The Eastman Legacy Collection, Rochester, NY.

Page 19. *Kodak camera magazine advertisement.* Print. 1890.

Page 21 (left inset). *J.P. Morgan.* Created by Pach Bros. Photographic Print. 1902. Now kept at the Library of Congress Prints and Photographs Division, Washington, DC.

Websites

Due to the changing nature of Internet links, The Rosen Publishing Group, Inc. has developed an online list of websites related to the subjects of this book. This site is updated regularly. Please use this link to access the list: **http://www.rcbmlinks.com/nysh/igny**